GCSE English AQA Anthology

The Workbook

Poems from Different Cultures

AQA A Specification — Foundation Level

This book is for anyone doing GCSE AQA Anthology at Foundation Level.

It contains lots of tricky questions designed to hone your poetry skills — because that's the only way you'll get any better.

It's also got some daft bits in to try and make the whole experience at least vaguely entertaining for you.

Edward Kamau Brathwaite

<u>Edward Kamau Brathwaite</u> was born in 1930 in Barbados in the West Indies. He's a poet and historian, and he's interested in links between slave nations and their African origins.

Limbo

And limbo stick is the silence in front of me
limbo

limbo
limbo like me
5 *limbo*
limbo like me

long dark night is the silence in front of me
limbo
limbo like me

10 stick hit sound
and the ship like it ready

stick hit sound
and the dark still steady

limbo
15 *limbo like me*

long dark deck and the water surrounding me
long dark deck and the silence is over me

limbo
limbo like me

20 stick is the whip
and the dark deck is slavery

stick is the whip
and the dark deck is slavery

limbo
25 *limbo like me*

drum stick knock
and the darkness is over me

knees spread wide
and the water is hiding

30 *limbo*
limbo like me

knees spread wide
and the dark ground is under me

down
35 down
down

and the drummer is calling me

limbo
limbo like me

40 sun coming up
and the drummers are praising me

out of the dark
and the dumb gods are raising me

up
45 up
up

and the music is saving me

hot
slow
50 step

on the burning ground.

© Edward Kamau Brathwaite 'Limbo' from *The Arrivants: A New World Trilogy* (OUP, 1973), reprinted by permission of Oxford University Press.

POEM DICTIONARY
Limbo has several meanings —
1. The West Indian dance, crouching backwards to pass under a horizontal stick — said to have originated from the experience of moving round in the cramped decks of slave ships
2. An imaginary place for the unwanted or forgotten
3. In Christianity, a place where infants who die before baptism go

Limbo

Q1 What does the phrase "knees spread wide" tell you about what it's like on the ship?

....

....

Q2 Give an example of imagery (visual descriptions) in the poem.

....

....

Q3 What effect does the rhythm of lines 10 and 12 have?

....

....

....

Q4 a) Why do you think the poet repeats the lines *"limbo limbo like me"*?

....

....

....

b) Find another example of repetition in the poem and describe the effect it has.

....

....

....

Q5 Pick out a phrase from the poem which stands out to you. Explain why you like or dislike it.

....

....

....

....

Section One — The Poems

Tatamkhulu Afrika

<u>Tatamkhulu Afrika</u> was born in Egypt in 1920 but raised as a white South African in District Six of Cape Town. When apartheid was introduced, he refused to be classed as a "superior" white. He joined the African National Congress (ANC) and was a political prisoner because of his fight against apartheid.

Nothing's Changed

Small round hard stones click
under my heels,
seeding grasses thrust
bearded seeds
5   into trouser cuffs, cans,
trodden on, crunch
in tall, purple-flowering,
amiable weeds.

District Six.
10 No board says it is:
but my feet know,
and my hands,
and the skin about my bones,
and the soft labouring of my lungs,
15 and the hot, white, inwards turning
anger of my eyes.

Brash with glass,
name flaring like a flag,
it squats
20 in the grass and weeds,
incipient Port Jackson trees:
new, up-market, haute cuisine,
guard at the gatepost,
whites only inn.

25 No sign says it is:
but we know where we belong.

I press my nose
to the clear panes, know,
before I see them, there will be
30 crushed ice white glass,
linen falls,
the single rose.

Down the road,
working man's cafe sells
35 bunny chows.
Take it with you, eat
it at a plastic table's top,
wipe your fingers on your jeans,
spit a little on the floor:
40 it's in the bone.

I back from the glass,
boy again,
leaving small mean O
of small, mean mouth.
45 Hands burn
for a stone, a bomb,
to shiver down the glass.
Nothing's changed.

<u>POEM DICTIONARY</u>
amiable — likeable / friendly
incipient — developing, just starting
Port Jackson trees — large pine trees
haute cuisine — high-class, expensive food
bunny chows — cheap food for the poor

Nothing's Changed

Q1 Complete the table below with phrases from the poem which show how the inn and the cafe differ.

	The inn	The cafe
Type of food		
Eating surface		
Hygiene / cleanliness		

Q2 What impression do you get of District Six from the descriptions in the first verse? What words give you this impression?

....
....
....

Q3 What effect do lines 10 and 25 have?

....
....
....
....

Q4 Why does the poet want to act violently at the end of the poem?

....
....
....

Q5 Now choose a phrase from the poem which stands out to you. Explain why you like or dislike it.

....
....
....
....

Section One — The Poems

Grace Nichols

Grace Nichols was born in Guyana in 1950. She was a journalist in the Caribbean until she moved to Britain in 1977. Both of these cultures and the ways they are connected are important to her.

Island Man

*(for a Caribbean island man in London who
still wakes up to the sound of the sea)*

Morning
and island man wakes up
to the sound of blue surf
in his head
5   the steady breaking and wombing

wild seabirds
and fishermen pushing out to sea
the sun surfacing defiantly
from the east
10   of his small emerald island
he always comes back   groggily groggily

Comes back to sands
of a grey metallic soar
                        to surge of wheels
15   to dull North Circular roar

muffling muffling
his crumpled pillow waves
island man heaves himself

Another London day

POEM DICTIONARY
North Circular — a busy London road

Section One — The Poems

Island Man

Q1   Find two phrases from the poem — one about the Caribbean and
      one about London — which show how their colours are different.

   Caribbean   ....

   London   ....

Q2   Which phrase is repeated on different lines to show that the man is gradually returning to reality?

   ....

Q3   How does the poet create the effect of being in a dream?

   ....

   ....

   ....

Q4   Describe the unusual layout on lines 11 and 14 and suggest why the poet has done this.

   ....

   ....

   ....

   ....

Q5   How do you think the man feels at the end of the poem? Give a relevant quote.

   ....

   ....

   ....

   ....

Q6   Now select a phrase from the poem which you can relate to and explain why you chose it.

   ....

   ....

   ....

   ....

Section One — The Poems

Imtiaz Dharker

<u>Imtiaz Dharker</u> was born in Pakistan in 1954. She has said that she believes identity comes from "beliefs and states of mind", rather than nationality or religion.

Blessing

The skin cracks like a pod.
There never is enough water.

Imagine the drip of it,
the small splash, echo
5   in a tin mug,
the voice of a kindly god.

Sometimes, the sudden rush
of fortune. The municipal pipe bursts,
silver crashes to the ground
10   and the flow has found
a roar of tongues. From the huts,
a congregation: every man woman
child for streets around
butts in, with pots,
15   brass, copper, aluminium,
plastic buckets,
frantic hands,

and naked children
screaming in the liquid sun,
20   their highlights polished to perfection,
flashing light,
as the blessing sings
over their small bones.

<u>POEM DICTIONARY</u>
municipal — to do with the city

Coordination Group Publications

AQA Anthology
Poems from Different Cultures

Answer Book

GCSE English
AQA A Specification — Foundation Level

The Answers

Contents

Section One Answers 2
Section Two Answers 6
Marking The Exam-Style Questions 8

A bullet point (•) before an answer means it's just a suggestion — either because there's more than one valid answer, or more than one way of correctly wording the answer.

Section One

Page 3 — Limbo

1. • "Knees spread wide" tells you that the ship is very cramped / uncomfortable because it suggests the ceilings were low and people had to kneel down, not stand.

2. • "burning ground"
   • "sun coming up"
   • "dumb gods are raising me"

3. • The short words and hard consonant sounds make you think of the cruelty of the beating given to the slaves.

4. a) • Repeating these lines sets a rhythm for the whole poem.
   b) • "up / up / up"
   The repetition suggests he has survived the voyage and is gradually leaving the misery of the slave ship behind him.

   The question asks you what the effect is, so you have to work out what impression the poet's trying to create.

5. • One phrase that stands out to me is "long dark night is the silence in front of me". I like it because it sums up how completely hopeless life as a slave must have been.

   You might find it tricky to find an expression that you think really, genuinely stands out from the rest of the poem. If this happens, try thinking about the overall feel of the poem, then find a line that you think sums this feeling up. No one will know you've answered the question backwards.

Page 5 — Nothing's Changed

1. •

	Type of food	Eating Surface	Hygiene / cleanliness
The cafe	"bunny chows"	"eat it at a plastic table's top"	"spit a little on the floor"
The inn	"haute cuisine"	"linen falls"	"crushed ice white glass"

2. • It seems neglected. Words like "hard stones", "weeds" and "cans, / trodden on" show the area needs lots of repair.

3. • These lines suggest that whites and blacks still don't mix in District Six, even though apartheid has officially ended.

   Remember to prove to the examiner that you know about the background of the poem.

4. • The poet wants to act violently because he is angry that black and white people are still separated in South Africa.

   Poems written in the first person like this one give you a good opportunity to try and see things from the poet's point of view.

5. • The phrase "I press my nose / to the clear panes" stands out to me. I like it because it shows clearly how the poet comes so close to the luxury of the inn but can't enter it because he's not white.

Page 7 — Island Man

1. Caribbean: "the sound of blue surf" or "emerald island"
   London: "grey metallic soar"

2. "Comes back"

   It's useful if you can spot a phrase like this that links the different bits of a poem together.

3. • The poet creates the impression of being in a dream by using the metaphor "pillow waves" and by saying that the sound of the sea is "in his head" rather than in reality.

4. • Lines 11 and 14 are separated from the rest of the text so they stand alone. Separating the words "groggily groggily" from the rest of the poem highlights that the man doesn't want to return to reality. Having "to surge of wheels" on its own shows the contrast between reality and the place he's been dreaming of.

5. • The man probably doesn't want to come back to reality. The phrase "heaves himself" suggests he is reluctantly returning to the reality of life in London.

6. • I like the phrase, "the sun surfacing defiantly". It makes the man's home island sound sunny and bright, so you feel sorry for him having to live in horrible London.

   It's quite possible you don't really feel sorry for the man. But it's often easier to go along with how the poet is trying to make you feel, rather than trying to come up with something really original under the pressure of the exam.

Page 9 — Blessing

1. • "kindly god"
   • "congregation"
   • "blessing"

2. a) • "frantic hands"
   b) • "the blessing sings"

3. • You can tell that water is very precious to the people in the poem because the poet compares it to "silver" — a valuable substance.

Answers

The Answers

4. • You can tell that the people in the poem usually struggle to get enough water, which would make life difficult for them. The phrase "Imagine the drip of it" shows us that it has been a long time since they have had any water at all.

5. • The items the slum dwellers use to collect the water show us how poor they are. The "pots" and "plastic buckets" sound like items grabbed quickly — it's all they have to collect the water.

   They must be desperate to collect as much water as possible, but all they've got are some pretty inefficient pots and buckets. So even though we're not told outright that they're poor, it's pretty obvious.

6. • I think the phrase "every man woman / child for streets around" is shocking because it shows how many people are thirsty. It really makes me realise how fortunate I am to always have water available.

Page 11 — Two Scavengers in a Truck, Two Beautiful People in a Mercedes

1. •

	The Scavengers	The Beautiful People
Their job	"garbagemen"	"his architect's office"
Their transport	"bright yellow garbage truck"	"elegant open Mercedes"
Their hair	"long hair" / "grey iron hair"	"casually coifed" / "shoulder-length blond hair"
Their clothes	"red plastic blazers"	"hip three-piece linen suit" / "short skirt colored stockings"

Look for phrases which highlight the differences between the rich couple and the poor scavengers — even though they're physically close together at the traffic light, they're socially far apart.

2. Any three words from the following: hip, downtown, cool, stoplight, garbagemen, back stoop
   Or other valid answers.

3. • By not using any full stops, the poem seems to describe a single, short moment in time.

4. • The poet has more sympathy for the garbagemen. He describes how they've been "up since four a.m.", which shows they've been working hard, whereas the rich couple haven't even got to work yet.

   Remember to use quotes. They show where you've got your ideas from.

5. • A phrase which stands out to me is "small gulf in the high seas of this democracy". This phrase is quite depressing, as if there's little hope of the distance between rich and poor getting any smaller.

   It might feel weird writing about your feelings and personal opinions in a workbook, but you'd better get used to it chum, because that's what's needed in the exam.

Page 13 — Night of the Scorpion

1. a) • "My mother twisted through and through"
   b) • "flash / of diabolic tail"
   The scorpion's also referred to as "the Evil One".

2. • The poet talks about reincarnation, which is an important part of Hinduism.
   You could also mention the holy man's incantation for this question.

3. • I think that using the a child's point of view makes the situation seem more confusing and frightening.

4. • Telling us that his father is a "sceptic" shows how desperate he is for the mother to recover. Even though he doesn't believe in all the religious 'cures', he still tries them out.

5. • The poet seems to think that all the religious cures are pointless. Near the end he simply says, "it lost its sting", which suggests that he expected this to happen all along, regardless of the religious cures.

6. • The phrase "giant scorpion shadows" stands out to me. It's a scary, evil image and it sums up how frightening the whole experience must have been for a child.

Page 15 — Vultures

1. •

	The Commandant	The vultures	
Ugliness	"hairy / nostrils"	"bashed-in head"	
Evil	"fumes of / human roast"	"cold / telescopic eyes"	
Kindness	"tender offspring"	"inclined affectionately"	

There's loads of descriptive stuff in this poem. These phrases make it nice and easy to compare the vultures and the Commandant.

2. • The phrase "if you will" asks the reader to consider the issues that the poet is raising.

3. • The poet creates a solemn mood in the poem by using dark and depressing language. For example, the phrase "greyness / and drizzle" is used to suggest a dark mood. Words like "ogre" and "evil" also create an unpleasant tone.

4. Both the vultures and the Commandant are disgusting and evil in general, but they are both still capable of affection.

   This is the main point of the poem. It might seem like there are two separate bits to the poem, but the stuff about the vultures is there to introduce the idea of human behaviour — so there are loads of comparisons between the two parts.

5. • I find the phrase "they picked / the eyes of a swollen / corpse" really disgusting. It shows just how horrible the vultures' eating habits are, and this is effective in highlighting how odd it is that they're still capable of tenderness.

   Remember, this poem's meant to be pretty grim. So don't go writing about how beautiful and charming the vultures' eating habits are — you'll just sound twisted and warped.

Answers

The Answers

Page 17 — What Were They Like?

1. • The poem uses a question and answer layout style. I think that the poet has chosen this form because it's structured and formal, which contrasts with the emotional content of the poem.

2. • "Stone" describes the lanterns that Vietnamese people used in Q1, but in A1 it is used to show that the Vietnamese people's hearts have been hardened by the war.

3. • The Vietnamese language is described as being beautiful — "singing resembled / the flight of moths in moonlight".

4. • The poem suggests that the Vietnamese people lived a happy, simple life. We are told that "peaceful clouds were reflected in the paddies," which suggests they lived peaceful lives.

5. • I find the phrase "after the children were killed" really shocking. It is said in a casual way, which suggests the people responsible for the children's deaths do not think it is very important.

Remember, there are no wrong answers to this kind of question. But whatever you say, you need to explain how the line you're talking about makes you feel.

Page 19 — Search For My Tongue

1. • The words in Gujarati create contrast in the poem. They show the difference between standard English and the author's "mother tongue".

2. a) The poet uses the metaphor of a tree / plant to represent her mother tongue.
   b) • It makes it seem as if her mother tongue is alive and growing inside her.

3. • The poet uses "you" and "I" to create an informal, conversational style to express her feelings.

4. • I think this is very important as it lets us appreciate how different Gujarati is to English. This helps to explain why the two tongues are in conflict in the first half of the poem.

Of course, you could say it's not very important, but it's harder to make a case for that. It's usually easier to say something's really effective — you generally come across as more interested in the poem that way.

5. • The phrase "it blossoms out of my mouth" appeals to me, because it's a happy phrase. It shows the poet is pleased that her mother tongue is still able to flow out of her mouth.

Page 21 — Unrelated Incidents

1. "Wanna yoo scruff"

2. a) "You wouldn't think it was true."
   b) "There's a right way to spell and a right way to talk."
   c) "You don't know the truth yourselves."

3. • A "BBC accent" means a middle-class, southern English way of speaking.

The poet refers to it as a "BBC accent" because it's the accent that BBC newsreaders traditionally speak in.

4. • The newsreader says that if the news were read in a regional accent, no one would believe it was the truth — "yi / widny thingk / it wuz troo".

5. • Writing in Scottish dialect allows the poet to use his own natural voice, showing he is not ashamed of it.

Remember, the poet disagrees strongly with the newsreader's view. So he mocks his attitude by "translating" it into his own dialect. So we hear someone saying that regional accents are inferior, in a regional accent. This adds humour to the poem.

6. • The phrase "thirza right / way ti spell" stands out to me because it contradicts itself. The newsreader is saying that regional dialects are incorrect, but the poet puts this opinion into Glaswegian dialect. This has a humorous effect because it shows he's mocking the people who don't like regional accents.

Page 23 — Half-Caste

1. i) • "when light an shadow / mix in de sky"
   ii) • "england weather / nearly always half-caste"

2. • The poet uses humour to make fun of people's attitudes towards mixed-race people. E.g. He makes fun of the term "half-caste" by saying he closes "half-a-eye". This is funny because it's a silly, impossible idea.

You have to show that you can recognise the bits that are meant to be funny, even if they're not exactly Reeves and Mortimer. And remember, the jokes aren't just there to try and make you laugh — they're there to show that the poet thinks something is stupid.

3. • The poet uses "I" and "yu" a lot. This lets him talk directly to the person he is arguing with and challenge their opinions, e.g. "Explain yuself". Also, he uses a dialect, which lets him be more direct than he could be if he used standard English.

4. • At the end of the poem the poet says that people must stop being narrow-minded before he will tell them everything about himself.

5. • I find the phrase "half-caste canvas" amusing. Referring to a painting as half-caste sounds strange, because it's the mix of colours that makes a painting interesting. So the phrase shows that mixtures are a good thing, not a bad thing.

In "Half-Caste", all the stuff about music and painting relates to what the poet says about being mixed-race. He is basically using different examples of how mixtures of things are natural and good.

Page 25 — Love After Love

1. i) • "Give wine. Give bread."
   ii) • "Feast on your life".

2. • The stranger in the poem is the bits of yourself that get forgotten when you are in a relationship with another person.

3. • The poet advises people to celebrate the fact that they are single: "Feast on your life".

Disclaimer: CGP does not endorse the advice of Derek Walcott. Feasting on one's own life can result in itchy skin and premature baldness.

4. • The love-letters and photographs are reminders of a relationship. The poet wants people to remove them so that they can get on with single life.

5. • The poet thinks being single is a good thing. He says, "Give back your heart / To itself," which sounds positive.

6. • I like the phrase "Give wine. Give bread". It gives the poem a ceremonial feel, suggesting that becoming single is important and something to celebrate.

It doesn't matter if the phrase you choose has already appeared in one of your answers. Also, it doesn't matter how long the phrase is — as long as it's more than one word and not half the poem or something silly.

Answers

The Answers

Page 27 — This Room

1. i) • "crash"
   ii) • "bang"
   iii) • "clang"

   These words add to the impression that the event described in the poem is loud and dramatic.

2. The room, the bed, chairs, furniture, pots and pans, garlic, onions, spices, her hands.

3. It means all the routines and habits of everyday life.

4. • The poet seems happy about what's happening, and she can't quite believe it. She says, "This is the time and place / to be alive", which shows how positive she is feeling.

5. • The room is described as being "in search of space, light / empty air." This seems to sum up how the poet has been feeling. It highlights how the poet has broken free from the boredom she has been feeling.

Page 29 — Presents from my Aunts in Pakistan

1. • "conflict"
   • "fractured"
   • "beggars"

2. a) • I think that the phrase means that the poet feels out of place. She doesn't feel like she is at home in England.

   b) • I think that the phrase means that the author is trying to "see herself" wearing the Pakistani clothes, as though she can't quite believe it's her.

3. • Her memories of Pakistan seem to be uncertain. She mostly relies on second-hand accounts like photographs and newspapers.

4. • The poet feels uncertain of her identity at the end of the poem. The expression "of no fixed nationality" suggests that she doesn't feel fully Pakistani or English.

   The Pakistani clothes make her think about a part of her background that she'd previously ignored.

5. • The poet describes herself as "alien in the sitting-room" when she tries on the Pakistani clothes. I like this because it is really effective in showing just how out-of-place the Pakistani clothes make her feel.

   Remember to try and give a personal response to the poem. Say what your attitude to it is, or how it makes you feel.

Page 31 — Not my Business

1. Personification.

2. • The title of the poem is ironic because the activities of the soldiers do become his business when they come to take him away.

   The poet has a clear, strong message in "Not my Business" — he wants people to stand up to the regime.

3. a) • This shows that these incidents are not unusual — they happen regularly.
   b) • This shows that he knows them. It suggests they could be his friends.

4. • Repeating these lines show that he hides behind this excuse — he's determined to ignore what's happening, no matter how many times it happens.

   These lines aren't there in the last verse, because now the person speaking them has become a victim himself.

5. • The phrase "A knock on the door froze my hungry hand" stands out to me, because it really shows how scared he is about the people coming to get him.

   If the poets don't say outright what emotions they're feeling, you need to work it out from the clues they give you.

Page 33 — Hurricane Hits England

1. • In 'Hurricane Hits England' the poet lies awake at night listening to a storm. The storm is violent, but it comforts her because it reminds her of the Caribbean, where she used to live.

2. The storm that hit England in October 1987.

3. Huracan, Oya and Shango are African storm gods.

4. • Before the storm, the poet felt homesick. She says there was a "frozen lake" inside her, which gives the impression that she was unhappy.

   The first two lines of the poem also suggest this. These clues about how she felt before are important for understanding the storm's effect on her.

5. • At the end of the poem the poet realises that everything on Earth is connected. This helps her to feel less homesick.

6. • The poet describes the "cratered graves" of the trees. I like this metaphor because it shows how huge the trees that were destroyed were, showing the power of the storm.

   If you quote a metaphor the poet's used, make sure you say why you think they've used it, and what effect it has.

The Answers

A bullet point (•) before an answer means it's just a suggestion — either because there's more than one valid answer, or more than one way of correctly wording the answer.

Section Two

Page 34 — Identity

1. • I'm a Scottish girl living in Edinburgh with my dad and brother. I'm fourteen and still at school. I only go to church at Christmas — my family isn't very religious. When I'm older I want to be a gardener — it's what I spend all my spare time doing.

   You don't have to write anything fancy for this question — just show you know the kind of things which make up identity (like your age, gender, where you live, family background and interests).

2. • In 'Hurricane Hits England' we see how identity can be related to where you're from. The woman realises that everywhere on Earth is linked: "the earth is the earth is the earth." The feeling that she's not so far from home after all makes her happier about herself.

   Identity is a big theme that could well come up in your exam. It's really useful to do practice questions like these which'll get you thinking about what identity means and how it relates to the poems you're studying.

Page 35 — Politics

1. • I would write a poem about sexism. This issue is important to me because I feel that women are under-represented in society — for example, there are only a small number of female MPs.

   It's worth having a think about what the theme means and how it affects your own life.

2. • In 'What Were They Like?', the poet describes the effects of the Vietnam war. She is very critical of this war. Her descriptions of its devastating effects on Vietnam — "after the children were killed" — show that she thinks the war was awful and cruel.

   Make sure you discuss what the poet's attitude is. You won't get many marks just for saying, "This poem is about the Vietnam War" — you have to talk about how the poet uses the descriptions in the poem to make a political point.

Page 36 — Change

1. • A big change happened in my life when my family moved house. I had to say goodbye to all my old friends and start a whole new life in the bright lights of Arbroath.

   We all have to face changes throughout our lives. It doesn't have to be something major.

2. • In 'Search For My Tongue', the poet experiences a positive change when she realises her mother tongue is still with her when she sleeps. She says "it grows back", and this realisation makes her happy and relieved.

   Like the other themes, "Change" covers a whole range of issues. The change could be good or bad, personal or shared, gradual or sudden.

Page 37 — People

1. • My best friend, Apple, is really important to me. I've known her since I was five. She has always been there for me when I've needed her; she was so supportive when my parents split up.

2. • In 'Night of the Scorpion', the child doesn't mix with the other people in the poem very much. He watches the events unfold but does not become involved.

   A good way of comparing poems from the 'People' point of view is to look at whether the people in the poems feel like they're part of a group, or as if it's just them on their own, against the world.

Page 38 — First Person

1. i) • Writing in the first person lets the poet describe how they're feeling much better than if they just used "he" or "she" all the time.

   ii) • It makes it easier to argue and persuade people, as the poet can make their points more directly.

2. • In 'Half-Caste', John Agard uses the first person so he can talk directly to the readers. He says "wha yu mean", which lets him challenge the beliefs of people who disagree with him.

   It's easy to spot which poems are written in the first person — it's the ones which have words like "me", "I", "my", and "mine" in them.

Page 39 — Specific Cultural References

1. • I really like the Cornish culture. I went on holiday to Cornwall last summer and we stayed in a traditional fishing village. The locals were really relaxed and friendly and the food was lovely — star-gazey pie every night.

2. • In 'Two Scavengers in a Truck...', the poet describes American culture. He shows that there's a big gap between rich and poor in America — there's a "small gulf" between the scavengers and the rich couple.

Page 40 — Description

1. • The funniest thing I ever saw was when our headmistress fell over a crisp packet on the stage in assembly. She was so gigantic that she rolled off the stage into the grand piano and broke it.

   Descriptions can involve personal memories. Look out for when poets do this.

2. • In 'Blessing', the poet's descriptions of the rush to collect water are very good at showing how desperate for water the people are. Phrases like "frantic hands" give an impression of the sudden rush of people from everywhere in the slum.

   Many poets show how they feel through the adjectives and metaphors they use, rather than stating their opinions outright.

Page 41 — Metaphor

1. i) • "silver crashes to the ground"

   ii) • "it grows back, a stump of a shoot / grows longer, grows moist...".

   Metaphors make a poem sound a bit more interesting.

2. • In 'Half-Caste' the poet uses metaphors to make fun of the description of people as "half-caste". He uses metaphors to compare himself to a painting that mixes "red and green". This pokes fun at the idea that the colour of his skin makes him an incomplete person.

   Remember — a metaphor is a description that says something is something else. Don't get it confused with similes — these say that something is like something else.

Answers

The Answers

Page 42 — Unusual Presentation

1. • A poet might use an unusual style of presentation to create a particular visual effect. This could be to highlight certain ideas or certain important lines in the poem.

2. • In 'Search For My Tongue', part of the poem is written in Gujarati (the poet's mother tongue). This makes it clear how different Gujarati looks and sounds to English, which helps to explain why the poet worries that she will forget how to speak her mother tongue.

If a poem's set out on the page in an odd way, it's not only to make it stand out. There'll be a specific reason why it looks like that — usually related to the poem's theme.

Page 43 — Non-Standard English

1. • "Non-standard English" means any form of English that is different from a posh, southern accent and standard forms of grammar.

Standard English accents are sometimes called "Received Pronunciation", or "The Queen's English".

2. • In 'Unrelated Incidents', the Glaswegian dialect is really important for getting across the poet's ideas to the reader. The theme of the poem is people's attitudes towards regional accents. So using expressions like "yi canny talk / right" helps poke fun at people who think regional accents are inferior.

In 'Unrelated Incidents', the whole poem is written in dialect. Look out for poems like 'Half-Caste', where the non-standard dialect is mixed in with standard English.

Page 44 — Particular Places

1. • My favourite place is Morecambe. It's got a big, old-fashioned sea front which is full of the sounds of seagulls and tourists. It's an exciting place which always brings back memories.

2. • In 'Nothing's Changed', the poet's descriptions of District Six make it seem wild and neglected. Phrases like the "Small round hard stones" make it seem like an unpleasant place to be, and the grasses and seeds suggest the streets are being taken over by weeds.

The physical appearance of District Six is important because it highlights the poet's opinion that nothing has been done to improve black people's lives.

Page 45 — Two Cultures

1. • I feel that I belong to just one culture. I have lived in Bradford all my life, and although my father is Welsh, I have never been there — I feel Yorkshire through and through.

2. • In 'Search For My Tongue', the poet feels that two cultures can't mix. The two cultures in her life are represented by languages. She says that her mother tongue "could not really know the other", suggesting that they will always be separate parts of her identity.

With the 'Two Cultures' theme, the poems generally fall into one of two camps — some say cultures can mix together, other say they clash. Picking one of each and then comparing them is a good idea for the exam questions.

Page 46 — Universal Ideas

1. • Last week I went to see 'The Day After Tomorrow'. The film really made me think about the issues surrounding global warming because it could change the world forever. I've decided that I'm going to make more journeys on my bike instead of asking my dad for a lift so I'll be making a little contribution to reducing global warming.

2. • The theme in 'Love After Love' is single life. The poet shows that it's a positive thing, by using words like "elation". No specific details are given, like names or places, so the poet's advice seems to apply to anyone at any time.

Some poets have a strong opinion and try to convince you that they're right, e.g. 'Love After Love' and 'Half-Caste'. Others are less certain, and just want to get people thinking about an issue, like in 'Vultures'.

Page 47 — Traditions

1. • Every summer after the last day of school, my friend Zainab and I go and play pooh sticks from the bridge by the park in our village. We've done this every year for as long as I can remember.

2. • In 'What Were They Like?', the poet creates a mysterious, positive impression of Vietnamese traditions. Although there is an uncertain tone, the suggestion of holding "ceremonies / to reverence the opening of buds" hints at ancient traditions.

As a general rule, if the poet describes a tradition in a positive or impressive way, they're demonstrating a connection with a culture or a place, in the past or in the present. Some poets, though, are more critical of traditions, like in 'Night of the Scorpion'.

Marking The Exam-Style Questions

There aren't any detailed answers to the exam-style questions here because there are loads of possible answers that would be equally valid. If you want a bit more guidance, have a look at CGP's Study Guide — it's got some example essays with plenty of useful notes.

This list tells you all the things you need to do to get a grade C in an exam essay. Read it carefully and try to do as many of these things as you can in your answers to the exam-style questions.

Then, when you've finished an answer, go back to this list and check how many of the things you've managed to do. If you've missed any out, then make an effort to include them in your next essay.

- Read the questions carefully and jot down some notes to plan your answer. When you start writing, make sure that you stick to answering the question — don't start waffling about stuff that just isn't relevant.

- Use quotes and specific details from the text in your answer whenever you can, to back up the points you make.

- Try and pick out more than one writing technique used by the writer, e.g. alliteration, similes, onomatopoeia. As well as knowing what the techniques are you need to explain why you think they've been chosen.

- Show that you understand what the author's ideas, attitudes and feelings about a particular issue are.

- Pay particular attention to the characters in the poem — you have to be able to show that you understand how the poet presents people.

- Mention the structure of the poem, especially if the presentation is unusual. Use specific details from the poem to back up your points.

- When you compare two poems, make sure you mention both poems roughly equally. So you need to make sure that every point you make refers to both poems.

- Finally, remember the basics. Make sure that your handwriting is neat — you won't get any marks if they can't read what you've written. Also, pay attention to your spelling, grammar and punctuation.

Answers

Blessing

Q1 Write down three words or phrases in the poem which are linked to religion.

i) .... ii) .... iii) ....

Q2 Find a phrase from the poem which suggests:

a) that the villagers are desperate to get at the spilt water. ....

b) that a miracle has happened. ....

Q3 How do you know that water is very precious to the people in the poem? Use a quote from the poem in your answer.

....

....

Q4 What impression do lines 1-6 give us of everyday life for the people in the poem? Support your answer with a relevant quote.

....

....

....

....

Q5 What is the effect of the descriptions of the items the people use to collect the water?

....

....

....

....

Q6 Now you're familiar with the poem, choose a phrase which stands out to you. Then explain why you like or dislike it.

....

....

....

....

Section One — The Poems

Lawrence Ferlinghetti

Lawrence Ferlinghetti was born in New York in 1919. He settled in San Francisco and is interested in how different cultures and races mix. He's concerned about the growing gap between rich and poor.

Two Scavengers in a Truck,
Two Beautiful People in a Mercedes

At the stoplight waiting for the light
                        nine a.m. downtown San Francisco
a bright yellow garbage truck
          with two garbagemen in red plastic blazers
5   standing on the back stoop
              one on each side hanging on
and looking down into
                an elegant open Mercedes
      with an elegant couple in it
10 The man
        in a hip three-piece linen suit
             with shoulder-length blond hair & sunglasses
The young blond woman so casually coifed
           with a short skirt and colored stockings
15   on the way to his architect's office

And the two scavengers up since four a.m.
                   grungy from their route
     on the way home
The older of the two with grey iron hair
20   and hunched back
    looking down like some
        gargoyle Quasimodo
And the younger of the two
        also with sunglasses & long hair
25 about the same age as the Mercedes driver

And both scavengers gazing down
                  as from a great distance
   at the cool couple
     as if they were watching some odorless TV ad
30   in which everything is always possible

And the very red light for an instant
     holding all four close together
  as if anything at all were possible
              between them
35   across that small gulf
      in the high seas
         of this democracy

POEM DICTIONARY
stoop — rear footplate of a truck
coifed — stylishly arranged hair
Quasimodo — the fictional hunchbacked bell ringer of Notre Dame
hip — fashionable
gargoyle — a carved monster on a church wall
odorless — with no smell (American spelling)

Two Scavengers in a Truck, Two Beautiful People in a Mercedes

Q1 There are loads of contrasts in this poem. Fill in the table below using words from the poem to show how different from each other the scavengers and the beautiful people are.

	The Scavengers	The Beautiful People
Their job		
Their transport		
Their hair		
Their clothes		

Q2 Write down three words in the poem which make you think of American culture and language.

i) .... ii) .... iii) ....

Q3 Why do you think the poet has chosen not to use any full stops?

....
....

Q4 Who does the poet have more sympathy for — the garbagemen or the couple in the Mercedes? Support your answer with a quote.

....
....
....
....

Q5 OK, like you've done before, pick out a phrase from the poem and explain why you like or dislike it.

....
....
....
....

Section One — The Poems

Nissim Ezekiel

Nissim Ezekiel was born in Bombay in 1924, to Jewish parents. But he was raised in a mainly Hindu culture, and has been influenced by atheist views.

Night of the Scorpion

I remember the night my mother
was stung by a scorpion. Ten hours
of steady rain had driven him
to crawl beneath a sack of rice.
5 Parting with his poison – flash
of diabolic tail in the dark room –
he risked the rain again.
The peasants came like swarms of flies
and buzzed the name of God a hundred times
10 to paralyse the Evil One.
With candles and with lanterns
throwing giant scorpion shadows
on the mud-baked walls
they searched for him: he was not found.
15 They clicked their tongues.
With every movement that the scorpion made
his poison moved in Mother's blood, they said.
May he sit still, they said.
May the sins of your previous birth
20 be burned away tonight, they said.
May your suffering decrease
the misfortunes of your next birth, they said.
May the sum of evil
balanced in this unreal world
25 against the sum of good
become diminished by your pain.
May the poison purify your flesh
of desire, and your spirit of ambition,
they said, and they sat around
30 on the floor with my mother in the centre,
the peace of understanding on each face.
More candles, more lanterns, more neighbours,
more insects, and the endless rain.
My mother twisted through and through,
35 groaning on a mat.
My father, sceptic, rationalist,
trying every curse and blessing,
powder, mixture, herb and hybrid.
He even poured a little paraffin
40 upon the bitten toe and put a match to it.
I watched the flame feeding on my mother.
I watched the holy man perform his rites
to tame the poison with an incantation.
After twenty hours
45 it lost its sting.

My mother only said
Thank God the scorpion picked on me
and spared my children.

POEM DICTIONARY
diabolic — to do with the devil
diminished — reduced
sceptic — a doubtful person
rationalist — a person who uses logical thinking to explain things
hybrid — a mixture of things
rites — actions in a ceremony
incantation — religious chanting

© Nissim Ezekiel 'Night of the Scorpion' from *Poverty Poems*, reproduced by permission of Oxford University Press India, New Delhi

Section One — The Poems

Night of the Scorpion

Q1   Write down a phrase from the poem which shows that:

   a)   the poet's mother is in pain.

   ....

   b)   the villagers associate the scorpion with the devil.

   ....

Q2   Pick out one idea from the Hindu religion which is mentioned in the poem.

   ....

   ....

Q3   Why do you think the author has chosen to write the poem from the point of view of a child?

   ....

   ....

Q4   The poet describes his father as a "sceptic" (line 36). Why is this important?

   ....

   ....

   ....

Q5   What do you think is the poet's attitude towards the neighbours' religious response? Support your answer with a quote.

   ....

   ....

   ....

Q6   Read through the poem again and write down the phrase that stands out the most to you. Explain why you like or dislike the phrase.

   ....

   ....

   ....

   ....

Section One — The Poems

Chinua Achebe

Chinua Achebe was born in Nigeria in 1931. He worked for the Nigerian Broadcasting Corporation, but when war broke out in 1967, he joined the government of Biafra (an area that violently split from the rest of Nigeria). He's written lots of poems about war and its effects.

Vultures

In the greyness
and drizzle of one despondent
dawn unstirred by harbingers
of sunbreak a vulture
5   perching high on broken
bone of a dead tree
nestled close to his
mate his smooth
bashed-in head, a pebble
10 on a stem rooted in
a dump of gross
feathers, inclined affectionately
to hers. Yesterday they picked
the eyes of a swollen
15 corpse in a water-logged
trench and ate the
things in its bowel. Full
gorged they chose their roost
keeping the hollowed remnant
20 in easy range of cold
telescopic eyes ...
      Strange
indeed how love in other
ways so particular
25 will pick a corner
in that charnel-house
tidy it and coil up there, perhaps
even fall asleep – her face
turned to the wall!

30 ... Thus the Commandant at Belsen
Camp going home for
the day with fumes of
human roast clinging
rebelliously to his hairy
35 nostrils will stop
at the wayside sweet-shop
and pick up a chocolate
for his tender offspring
waiting at home for Daddy's
40 return...
      Praise bounteous
providence if you will
that grants even an ogre
a tiny glow-worm
45 tenderness encapsulated
in icy caverns of a cruel
heart or else despair
for in the very germ
of that kindred love is
50 lodged the perpetuity
of evil.

POEM DICTIONARY
harbinger — a messenger / a sign of things to come
charnel-house — a place where corpses are stored
Commandant — a commanding officer
Belsen — a Nazi concentration camp
bounteous providence — the good things that God has given to mankind
encapsulated — enclosed
perpetuity — lasting forever

Section One — The Poems

Vultures

Q1 Fill in the table below with phrases from the poem that describe the different qualities of the vultures and the Commandant.

	The vultures	The Commandant
Ugliness		
Evil		
Kindness		

Q2 What is the purpose of the phrase "if you will" (line 42)?

....
....

Q3 Explain how the poet creates a solemn mood in the poem. Use quotes from the poem in your answer.

....
....
....
....

Q4 What connections does the poet see between the vultures and the Commandant?

....
....
....

Q5 No surprise here — pick out a phrase from the poem which stands out to you. Explain why you like or dislike it.

....
....
....
....

Section One — The Poems

Denise Levertov

Denise Levertov (1923-97) was born in England but moved to New York in 1947. She later became an American citizen, but was strongly opposed to the USA's involvement in the Vietnam War.

What Were They Like?

1) Did the people of Viet Nam
   use lanterns of stone?
2) Did they hold ceremonies
   to reverence the opening of buds?
3) Were they inclined to quiet laughter?
4) Did they use bone and ivory,
   jade and silver, for ornament?
5) Had they an epic poem?
6) Did they distinguish between speech and singing?

1) Sir, their light hearts turned to stone.
   It is not remembered whether in gardens
   stone lanterns illumined pleasant ways.
2) Perhaps they gathered once to delight in blossom,
   but after the children were killed
   there were no more buds)
3) Sir, laughter is bitter to the burned mouth.
4) A dream ago, perhaps. Ornament is for joy.
   All the bones were charred.
5) It is not remembered. Remember,
   most were peasants; their life
   was in rice and bamboo.
   When peaceful clouds were reflected in the paddies
   and the water buffalo stepped surely along terraces,
   maybe fathers told their sons old tales.
   When bombs smashed those mirrors
   there was time only to scream.
6) There is an echo yet
   of their speech which was like a song.
   It was reported that their singing resembled
   the flight of moths in moonlight.
   Who can say? It is silent now.

© 'What Were They Like?' from Selected Poems (Bloodaxe Books, 1986).
Reproduced by permission of Pollinger Limited and the proprietor.

POEM DICTIONARY
reverence — deep respect or worship
jade — a gemstone, normally green
illumined — lit up
charred — blackened by fire
paddies — waterlogged fields for growing rice
terraces — different levels of fields for farming

Section One — The Poems

What Were They Like?

Q1 What layout style does this poem take? Suggest a reason why the author chose this style.

....
....
....
....

Q2 Find a word which has different meanings in different parts of the poem and explain how its meaning changes.

....
....
....

Q3 How is the Vietnamese language described? Use a quote from the poem to back up you answer.

....
....
....

Q4 What impression does the poem give us of the Vietnamese way of life before the war? Explain your answer with a relevant quote.

....
....
....

Q5 It's time for you to pick out a phrase. Don't forget to explain how it makes you feel.

....
....
....
....

Section One — The Poems

Sujata Bhatt

<u>Sujata Bhatt</u> was born in India in 1956, later lived in the USA and now lives in Germany with her husband. She writes in both English and Gujarati, her mother tongue.

from Search For My Tongue

You ask me what I mean
by saying I have lost my tongue.
I ask you, what would you do
if you had two tongues in your mouth,
5   and lost the first one, the mother tongue,
and could not really know the other,
the foreign tongue.
You could not use them both together
even if you thought that way.
10   And if you lived in a place you had to
speak a foreign tongue,
your mother tongue would rot,
rot and die in your mouth,
until you had to spit it out.
15   I thought I spit it out
but overnight while I dream,
મને હતું કે આખ્ખી જીભ આખ્ખી ભાષા,
(munay hutoo kay aakhee jeebh aakhee bhasha)
મેં થૂંકી નાખી છે.
20   (may thoonky nakhi chay)
પરંતુ રાત્રે સ્વપ્નમાં મારી ભાષા પાછી આવે છે.
(parantoo rattray svupnama mari bhasha pachi aavay chay)
ફૂલની જેમ મારી ભાષા મારી જીભ
(foolnee jaim mari bhasha mari jeebh)
25   મોઢામાં ખીલે છે.
(modhama kheelay chay)
ફૂલની જેમ મારી ભાષા મારી જીભ
(fullnee jaim mari bhasha mari jeebh)
મોઢામાં પાકે છે.
30   (modhama pakay chay)
it grows back, a stump of a shoot
grows longer, grows moist, grows strong veins,
it ties the other tongue in knots,
the bud opens, the bud opens in my mouth,
35   it pushes the other tongue aside.
Everytime I think I've forgotten,
I think I've lost the mother tongue,
it blossoms out of my mouth.

<u>POEM DICTIONARY</u>
mother tongue — a person's first language

Search For My Tongue

Q1 What effect do the Gujarati words have on the visual appearance of the poem?

....

....

Q2 a) What metaphor does the poet use to represent her mother tongue?

....

....

b) What effect do you think the poet is trying to create by using this metaphor?

....

....

....

Q3 Why do you think the poet uses the words "you" and "I" a lot?

....

....

....

Q4 In lines 17-30, we "hear" the Gujarati language. How important do you think this is to the impact of the poem? Explain your answer.

....

....

....

Q5 Now choose a phrase from the poem which appeals to you and explain why you like or dislike it.

....

....

....

....

Section One — The Poems

Tom Leonard

Tom Leonard was born in Glasgow in 1944. He's often written about people's attitudes to different accents, and says he writes in Scottish dialect so that his 'voice' can be heard through his poetry.

from **Unrelated Incidents**

this is thi
six a clock
news thi
man said n
5   thi reason
a talk wia
BBC accent
iz coz yi
widny wahnt
10 mi ti talk
aboot thi
trooth wia
voice lik
wanna yoo
15 scruff. if
a toktaboot
thi trooth
lik wanna yoo
scruff yi
20 widny thingk
it wuz troo.
jist wanna yoo
scruff tokn.
thirza right
25 way ti spell
ana right way
ti tok it. this
is me tokn yir
right way a
30 spellin. this
is ma trooth
yooz doant no
thi trooth
yirsellz cawz
35 yi canny talk
right. this is
the six a clock
nyooz. belt up.

Unrelated Incidents

Q1 Which repeated phrase suggests the newsreader looks down on working-class people?

....

Q2 Re-write these phrases from the poem into standard English.

a) "yi widny thingk it wuz troo"

....

b) "thirza right way ti spell ana right way ti tok it"

....

c) "yooz doant no thi trooth yirsellz"

....

Q3 What is meant by the phrase "BBC accent"?

....

Q4 Why does the newsreader think that the news shouldn't be read in a regional accent? Support your answer with a quote.

....
....
....

Q5 Why do you think the poet has chosen to put the newsreader's words into Scottish dialect?

....
....
....

Q6 Choose a phrase from the poem that you find interesting. Explain why you chose it.

....
....
....

Section One — The Poems

John Agard

John Agard was born in Guyana in South America in 1949, to parents of mixed nationality. He came to Britain in 1977. He likes to perform his poems, and believes humour is an effective way of challenging people's opinions.

Half-Caste

Excuse me
standing on one leg
I'm half-caste

Explain yuself
5   wha yu mean
when yu say half-caste
yu mean when picasso
mix red an green
is a half-caste canvas/
10 explain yuself
wha yu mean
when yu say half-caste
yu mean when light an shadow
mix in de sky
15 is a half-caste weather/
well in dat case
england weather
nearly always half-caste
in fact some o dem cloud
20 half-caste till dem overcast
so spiteful dem dont want de sun pass
ah rass/
explain yuself
wha yu mean
25 when yu say half-caste
yu mean tchaikovsky
sit down at dah piano
an mix a black key
wid a white key
30 is a half-caste symphony/

Explain yuself
wha yu mean
Ah listening to yu wid de keen
half of mih ear
35 Ah lookin at yu wid de keen
half of mih eye
and when I'm introduced to yu
I'm sure you'll understand
why I offer yu half-a-hand
40 an when I sleep at night
I close half-a-eye
consequently when I dream
I dream half-a-dream
an when moon begin to glow
45 I half-caste human being
cast half-a-shadow
but yu must come back tomorrow
wid de whole of yu eye
an de whole of yu ear
50 an de whole of yu mind

an I will tell yu
de other half
of my story

POEM DICTIONARY
Picasso — the name of a 20th Century Spanish painter
Tchaikovsky — the name of a 19th Century Russian classical music composer

Half-Caste

Q1   Give two examples of imagery used in the poem.

   i) ....

   ii) ....

Q2   How does the poet use humour to get his point across? Support your answer with a quote.

   ....
   ....
   ....
   ....

Q3   How does the poet create an argumentative tone? Include quotes in your answer.

   ....
   ....
   ....
   ....

Q4   At the end of the poem (lines 47-53) what does the poet say people must do before he will tell them "de other half" of his story? Explain what he means in your own words.

   ....
   ....
   ....
   ....

Q5   Which phrase in the poem stands out to you the most? Explain why you like or dislike it.

   ....
   ....
   ....
   ....

Section One — The Poems

Derek Walcott

Derek Walcott was born in St Lucia, in the West Indies, in 1930. His father was English and his mother was African. As well as poetry, he's written plays, and is a painter.

Love After Love

The time will come
When, with elation,
You will greet yourself arriving
At your own door, in your own mirror,
5   And each will smile at the other's welcome,

And say sit here. Eat.
You will love again the stranger who was your self.
Give wine. Give bread. Give back your heart
To itself, to the stranger who has loved you

10   All your life, whom you ignored
For another, who knows you by heart.
Take down the love-letters from the bookshelf

The photographs, the desperate notes,
Peel your own images from the mirror.
15   Sit. Feast on your life.

Love After Love

Q1   Give two examples of religious / ceremonial language in the poem.

   i) ....

   ii) ....

Q2   Who is the "stranger" that the poet talks about?

   ....

   ....

Q3   What does the poet tell the reader to celebrate? Use a quote from the poem in your answer.

   ....

   ....

   ....

Q4   Why does the poet advise the reader to take down their love-letters and photographs?

   ....

   ....

   ....

Q5   Does the poet think being single is a good or bad thing? Support your answer with a quote.

   ....

   ....

   ....

   ....

Q6   Now choose a phrase from the poem that stands out to you. Explain why you like or dislike it.

   ....

   ....

   ....

   ....

Section One — The Poems

Imtiaz Dharker

Imtiaz Dharker was born in Pakistan in 1954. She has said that she believes identity comes from "beliefs and states of mind", rather than nationality or religion.

This Room

This room is breaking out
of itself, cracking through
its own walls
in search of space, light,
5   empty air.

The bed is lifting out of
its nightmares.
From dark corners, chairs
are rising up to crash through clouds.

10   This is the time and place
to be alive:
when the daily furniture of our lives
stirs, when the improbable arrives.
Pots and pans bang together
15   in celebration, clang
past the crowd of garlic, onions, spices,
fly by the ceiling fan.
No one is looking for the door.

In all this excitement
20   I'm wondering where
I've left my feet, and why

my hands are outside, clapping.

POEM DICTIONARY
improbable — unlikely, incredible

Section One — The Poems

This Room

Q1 Write down three examples of onomatopoeia from the poem.

i) ....

ii) ....

iii) ....

Onomatopoeia is when words sound like the thing they're describing e.g "crunch".

Q2 Make a list of objects that are personified (given human qualities) in this poem.

....

....

....

Q3 What do you think "the daily furniture of our lives" means?

....

....

....

Q4 How do you think the poet feels about what is happening? Support your answer with a quote.

....

....

....

....

Q5 Choose a phrase from the poem that interests you — explain why you chose it.

....

....

....

....

Section One — The Poems

Moniza Alvi

<u>Moniza Alvi</u> was born in Pakistan in 1954, to a Pakistani father and an English mother. She moved to England as a child, and revisited Pakistan for the first time in 1993.

Presents from my Aunts in Pakistan

They sent me a salwar kameez
    peacock-blue,
        and another
    glistening like an orange split open,
5 embossed slippers, gold and black
        points curling.
    Candy-striped glass bangles
      snapped, drew blood.
    Like at school, fashions changed
10   in Pakistan –
the salwar bottoms were broad and stiff,
      then narrow.
My aunts chose an apple-green sari,
    silver-bordered
15   for my teens.

I tried each satin-silken top –
    was alien in the sitting-room.
I could never be as lovely
        as those clothes –
20   I longed
for denim and corduroy.
    My costume clung to me
        and I was aflame,
I couldn't rise up out of its fire,
25   half-English,
      unlike Aunt Jamila.

I wanted my parents' camel-skin lamp –
    switching it on in my bedroom,
to consider the cruelty
30   and the transformation
from camel to shade,
    marvel at the colours
      like stained glass.

My mother cherished her jewellery –
35   Indian gold, dangling, filigree.
        But it was stolen from our car.
The presents were radiant in my wardrobe.
    My aunts requested cardigans
      from Marks and Spencers.

40 My salwar kameez
      didn't impress the schoolfriend
who sat on my bed, asked to see
    my weekend clothes.
But often I admired the mirror-work,
45   tried to glimpse myself
        in the miniature
glass circles, recall the story
    how the three of us
        sailed to England.
50 Prickly heat had me screaming on the way.
    I ended up in a cot
in my English grandmother's dining-room,
    found myself alone,
        playing with a tin boat.

55 I pictured my birthplace
    from fifties' photographs.
        When I was older
there was conflict, a fractured land
    throbbing through newsprint.
60 Sometimes I saw Lahore –
        my aunts in shaded rooms,
screened from male visitors,
    sorting presents,
        wrapping them in tissue.

65 Or there were beggars, sweeper-girls
    and I was there –
        of no fixed nationality,
staring through fretwork
    at the Shalimar Gardens.

<u>POEM DICTIONARY</u>
salwar kameez — Pakistani items of clothing
Lahore — a city in Pakistan
Shalimar Gardens — peaceful, walled gardens in Lahore
filigree — delicate gold jewellery
fretwork — metal bars for decoration

Section One — The Poems

Presents from my Aunts in Pakistan

Q1   Write down three words in the poem which suggest a negative image of Pakistan.

   i) ....   ii) ....   iii) ....

Q2   Explain what you think the following phrases mean:

   a)   "was alien in the sitting-room"

   ....

   ....

   ....

   b)   "I admired the mirror-work, tried to glimpse myself in the minature glass circles"

   ....

   ....

   ....

Q3   How clear are the poet's memories of Pakistan? Explain your answer.

   ....

   ....

   ....

Q4   How does the poet feel about her identity at the end of the poem? Support your answer with a quote.

   ....

   ....

   ....

   ....

Q5   Write down a phrase from the poem that grabs your attention.
   Briefly explain why you like or dislike it.

   ....

   ....

   ....

   ....

Section One — The Poems

Niyi Osundare

Niyi Osundare was born in Nigeria in 1947, and is a Professor of English. He has often spoken out against military regimes in his home country.

Not my Business

They picked Akanni up one morning
Beat him soft like clay
And stuffed him down the belly
Of a waiting jeep.
5   What business of mine is it
          So long they don't take the yam
          From my savouring mouth?

They came one night
Booted the whole house awake
10 And dragged Danladi out,
Then off to a lengthy absence.
          What business of mine is it
          So long they don't take the yam
          From my savouring mouth?

15 Chinwe went to work one day
Only to find her job was gone:
No query, no warning, no probe –
Just one neat sack for a stainless record.
          What business of mine is it
20   So long they don't take the yam
          From my savouring mouth?

And then one evening
As I sat down to eat my yam
A knock on the door froze my hungry hand.
25 The jeep was waiting on my bewildered lawn
Waiting, waiting in its usual silence.

POEM DICTIONARY
yam — vegetable eaten in hot countries

Section One — The Poems

Not my Business

Q1 What poetic device does the author use to describe the jeep and the lawn?

....

Q2 Why is the title of the poem ironic?

Irony is when the writer says one thing but means something else. It's a way of being sarcastic or funny.

....

....

....

Q3 Why do you think the poet:

a) mentions the time of day in the first line of each verse?

....

....

b) describes the victims by their first names?

....

....

Q4 What effect do the three lines that are repeated have?

....

....

....

....

Q5 Look over the poem again and pick out the phrase that stands out to you most. Explain what effect it has on you.

....

....

....

....

Section One — The Poems

Grace Nichols

Grace Nichols was born in Guyana in 1950. She now lives and writes in Sussex.

Hurricane Hits England

It took a hurricane, to bring her closer
To the landscape.
Half the night she lay awake,
The howling ship of the wind,
5 Its gathering rage,
Like some dark ancestral spectre.
Fearful and reassuring.

Talk to me Huracan
Talk to me Oya
10 Talk to me Shango
And Hattie,
My sweeping, back-home cousin.

Tell me why you visit
An English coast?
15 What is the meaning
Of old tongues
Reaping havoc
In new places?

The blinding illumination,
20 Even as you short-
Circuit us
Into further darkness?

What is the meaning of trees
Falling heavy as whales
25 Their crusted roots
Their cratered graves?

O why is my heart unchained?

Tropical Oya of the Weather,
I am aligning myself to you,
30 I am following the movement of your winds,
I am riding the mystery of your storm.

Ah, sweet mystery,
Come to break the frozen lake in me,
Shaking the foundations of the very trees within me,
35 Come to let me know
That the earth is the earth is the earth.

POEM DICTIONARY
ancestral spectre —
a ghost of the past
Huracan, Oya, Shango —
African storm gods

Hurricane Hits England

Q1 In your own words, write a summary of what happens in the poem.

....

....

....

....

Q2 What real-life event is the poem based on?

....

Q3 What are Huracan, Oya and Shango?

....

....

Q4 How has the character in the poem been feeling before the storm? Use a quotation in your answer.

....

....

....

....

Q5 What do you think the last line of the poem means?

....

....

....

Q6 For one last time — choose a phrase that stands out to you in the poem and explain why you like or dislike it.

....

....

....

....

Section One — The Poems

Identity

These Poems are about Identity:

Limbo (pages 2-3)
Nothing's Changed (pages 4-5)
Island Man (pages 6-7)
Search For My Tongue (pages 18-19)
Unrelated Incidents (pages 20-21)
Half-Caste (pages 22-23)
Love After Love (pages 24-25)
This Room (pages 26-27)
Presents from my Aunts in Pakistan (pages 28-29)
Hurricane Hits England (pages 32-33)

Q1 Write a couple of sentences about your identity.

....
....
....
....

Q2 Choose a poem that you know from the top of the page.
What does this poem say about what people think about themselves?

....
....
....
....
....

EXAM-STYLE QUESTION

Q3 Our identity comes from different parts of our culture. Compare and contrast how the poets examine the idea of identity in 'Search For My Tongue' and one other poem.

Compare:
- the language devices used
- the feelings and attitudes in the poems
- your opinion of each poem.

EXAM-STYLE QUESTION

Q4 Compare the ways the poets deal with identity in 'Limbo' and one other poem.

Compare:
- how the past is used
- the use of poetic devices
- the feelings expressed
- your opinion of each poem.

Politics

These Poems are about Politics:

Nothing's Changed (pages 4-5)
Two Scavengers in a Truck... (pages 10-11)
Vultures (pages 14-15)
What Were They Like? (pages 16-17)
Unrelated Incidents (pages 20-21)
Not my Business (pages 30-31)

Q1   If you were to write a poem about a political issue, which issue would you choose, and why?

....
....
....
....

Q2   Choose a poem from the top of the page that you know well.
What political situation does the poet describe, and what is his / her attitude towards it?

....
....
....
....
....

EXAM-STYLE QUESTION

Q3   Compare the political ideas presented in 'Two Scavengers in a Truck, Two Beautiful People in a Mercedes' and one other poem.

Compare:
- how they address divisions in society
- the language and layout used
- the attitudes expressed.

EXAM-STYLE QUESTION

Q4   Compare the ways that the poets show how political systems can treat people unfairly in 'Not my Business' and one other poem.

Compare:
- the inequality described
- the language used to describe them
- the feelings and attitudes expressed.

Section Two — The Themes

Change

These Poems are about Change:

Nothing's Changed (pages 4-5)
Blessing (pages 8-9)
What Were They Like? (pages 16-17)
Search For My Tongue (pages 18-19)
Love After Love (pages 24-25)
This Room (pages 26-27)
Presents from my Aunts in Pakistan (pages 28-29)

Q1 Write a couple of sentences about a change that has happened in your life.

....
....
....
....

Q2 Choose a poem that you know from the top of the page.
Describe the change that happens in this poem.

....
....
....
....
....

EXAM-STYLE QUESTION

Q3 Compare the ways the poets describe change in 'This Room' and one other poem.
Compare:
- whether the change described is a good thing or a bad thing
- the poetic devices used to describe the change
- the feelings connected to the change.

EXAM-STYLE QUESTION

Q4 'What Were They Like?' discusses changes caused by war.
Compare 'What Were They Like' with another poem that discusses negative change.
Compare:
- the changes that take place
- how layout is used
- the feelings and attitudes in the poems.

Section Two — The Themes

People

These Poems are about specific People:

Island Man (pages 6-7)
Two Scavengers in a Truck... (pages 10-11)
Night of the Scorpion (pages 12-13)
Vultures (pages 14-15)

Search For My Tongue (pages 18-19)
Half-Caste (pages 22-23)
Presents from my Aunts in Pakistan (pages 28-29)
Not my Business (pages 30-31)
Hurricane Hits England (pages 32-33)

Q1 Write a paragraph about a person or group of people who are important to you.

....
....
....
....

Q2 Choose a character or group of characters from one of the poems at the top of the page. How does this person / do these people mix with other people in the poem?

....
....
....
....
....

EXAM-STYLE QUESTION

Q3 'Hurricane Hits England' is about a person who feels homesick.
Compare the ways people are presented in 'Hurricane Hits England' and one other poem.

Compare:
- what the reader learns about the people in the poem
- the language devices used
- the feelings expressed in the poems.

EXAM-STYLE QUESTION

Q4 Compare the ways that people and their community are described in 'Two Scavengers in a Truck, Two Beautiful People in a Mercedes' and one other poem.

Compare:
- whether the descriptions are positive or negative
- the poetic devices used to describe them
- the poets' attitudes towards society.

Section Two — The Themes

First Person

These Poems use the First Person:

Nothing's Changed (pages 4-5)
Night of the Scorpion (pages 12-13)
Search For My Tongue (pages 18-19)
Half-Caste (pages 22-23)

This Room (pages 26-27)
Presents from my Aunts in Pakistan (pages 28-29)
Not my Business (pages 30-31)
Hurricane Hits England (pages 32-33)

Q1 Describe two reasons why you think a poet might decide to write in the first person.

i) ....
....

ii) ....
....

Q2 Yep, it's time for another of these questions — choose a poem that you know from the top of the page. How does using the first person make the poem's message more effective?

....
....
....
....
....

EXAM-STYLE QUESTION Q3 The use of the first person in 'Search For My Tongue' helps us understand the poet's thoughts and feelings. Compare how the first person is used in 'Search For My Tongue' and one other poem.

Compare:
- what the poems are about
- the feelings expressed
- the poets' reasons for writing in the first person.

EXAM-STYLE QUESTION Q4 The voice we hear in 'Nothing's Changed' is very angry. Compare this poem with one other poem that uses the first person to convey the feelings and attitudes of the poet.

Compare:
- what the poets are trying to say
- how the first person is used
- the feelings and attitudes in the poems
- your opinion of the ideas in the poems.

Section Two — The Themes

Specific Cultural References

These Poems have Specific Cultural References:

Limbo (pages 2-3)
Nothing's Changed (pages 4-5)
Two Scavengers in a Truck... (pages 10-11)
Night of the Scorpion (pages 12-13)
What Were They Like? (pages 16-17)

Search For My Tongue (pages 18-19)
Presents from my Aunts in Pakistan (pages 28-29)
Not my Business (pages 30-31)
Hurricane Hits England (pages 32-33)

Q1 Describe a culture that you feel part of, or that you have experienced.

....
....
....
....

Q2 See those poems in the box at the top? Pick one.
In this poem, which culture does the poet describe, and what impression do we get of this culture?

....
....
....
....
....
....

Q3 [EXAM-STYLE QUESTION] 'Two Scavengers in a Truck, Two Beautiful People in a Mercedes' describes the gap between the rich and poor of San Francisco. Choose another poem that uses specific cultural references and compare it with 'Two Scavengers...'

Compare:
- the cultural details that are described
- the attitudes of the poets
- the poets' reasons for using specific cultural references.

Q4 [EXAM-STYLE QUESTION] Compare the use of specific cultural references in 'Hurricane Hits England' and one other poem.

Compare:
- the different cultural details that are described
- the language devices used
- the poets' feelings about the cultures they describe.

Section Two — The Themes

Description

These Poems use Description a lot:
Nothing's Changed (pages 4-5)
Island Man (pages 6-7)
Blessing (pages 8-9)
Two Scavengers in a Truck... (pages 10-11)
Night of the Scorpion (pages 12-13)
Presents from my Aunts in Pakistan (pages 28-29)

Q1 Think about the funniest thing you've ever seen. Describe it in a brilliant and poetic way.

....
....
....
....

Q2 Pick a poem. A real beauty. One you know well. One from the box at the top of the page. How effective do you think the poet's descriptions are?

....
....
....
....
....
....

EXAM-STYLE QUESTION Q3 Compare the ways the poets describe particular places in 'Nothing's Changed' and one other poem.

Compare:
- the poets' attitudes towards the places described
- the use of poetic devices to create a particular impression of a place
- whether the place described is unique.

EXAM-STYLE QUESTION Q4 Traditional Pakistani clothes are described in 'Presents from my Aunts in Pakistan'. Compare 'Presents...' with one other poem that uses interesting descriptions.

Compare:
- how the poet uses poetic devices to create a particular impression
- the poets' feelings towards who/what is being described
- whether the descriptions are important to the poem's overall impact or not, and why.

Section Two — The Themes

Metaphor

These Poems use Metaphors:

Blessing (pages 8-9)
Vultures (pages 14-15)
Search For My Tongue (pages 18-19)

Half-Caste (pages 22-23)
This Room (pages 26-27)

Metaphors are a way of describing things by saying that they are something else e.g. "my car is a heap of old rubbish".

Q1 Write down metaphors from two of the poems in the list above.

i) ....

....

ii) ....

....

Q2 Sorry if this is getting a bit repetitive but I'm afraid that's just the way it is.
Select a poem from that box up there and explain why the poet's use of metaphors is effective.

....

....

....

....

....

EXAM-STYLE QUESTION

Q3 Compare the use of metaphors in 'This Room' and one other poem.

Compare:
- the types of metaphor used
- what feelings and attitudes are expressed by the metaphors
- how important you think the metaphors are to the overall impact of the poems.

EXAM-STYLE QUESTION

Q4 Compare the use of metaphors in 'Vultures' and one other poem.

Compare:
- what the poems are about
- the different uses and effects of metaphors
- how effective you think the metaphors are.

Section Two — The Themes

Unusual Presentation

These Poems have Unusual Presentation:

Limbo (pages 2-3)
Nothing's Changed (pages 4-5)
Island Man (pages 6-7)
Two Scavengers in a Truck... (pages 10-11)

What Were They Like? (pages 16-17)
Search For My Tongue (pages 18-19)
Unrelated Incidents (pages 20-21)
Presents from my Aunts in Pakistan (pages 28-29)

Q1 Why do you think a poet might decide to use an unusual style of presentation?

....
....
....
....

Q2 Explain what effect the style of presentation has in one of the poems that you are familiar with from the box above.

....
....
....
....
....

Q3 [EXAM-STYLE QUESTION] Compare 'What Were They Like?' with one other poem that has unusual presentation.

Compare:
- the effect the poets are trying to create by using this style of presentation
- the feelings and attitudes expressed in the poem
- how important you think the style of presentation is to the poems' message.

Q4 [EXAM-STYLE QUESTION] 'Unrelated Incidents' has a very unusual shape on the page. Compare this with one other poem that uses unusual presentation.

Compare:
- what the poems are about
- the feelings or ideas expressed in the poems
- how they use unusual presentation to express these feelings or ideas
- your opinion of each poem.

Section Two — The Themes

Non-Standard English

These Poems use Non-Standard English:

Limbo (pages 2-3)   Unrelated Incidents (pages 20-21)
Island Man (pages 6-7)   Half-Caste (pages 22-23)

Q1   What is "non-standard English"?

   ....
   ....
   ....
   ....

Q2   I imagine you've got the gist by now... choose a poem that you know from the top of the page. Why do you think the poet has chosen to write in non-standard English in this poem?

   ....
   ....
   ....
   ....
   ....

EXAM-STYLE QUESTION

Q3   Non-standard English is used in some poems to show the cultural background of the poets. Compare the use of non-standard English in 'Limbo' and one other poem.

   Compare:
   - the cultural backgrounds
   - the feelings expressed in the poems
   - how and why non-standard English is used to express these feelings.

EXAM-STYLE QUESTION

Q4   Compare the use of non-standard English in 'Unrelated Incidents' and one other poem.

   Compare:
   - the feelings or ideas expressed in the poems
   - how and why non-standard English is used
   - how effective you think the use of non-standard English is in the two poems.

Section Two — The Themes

Particular Places

These Poems are about Particular Places:

Nothing's Changed (pages 4-5)
Island Man (pages 6-7)
Two Scavengers in a Truck... (pages 10-11)
Vultures (pages 14-15)
What Were They Like? (16-17)
Presents from my Aunts in Pakistan (pages 28-29)
Hurricane Hits England (pages 32-33)

Q1 Write a couple of sentences to describe your favourite place.

....
....
....
....

Q2 Right, it's time to choose another poem from the blue box of destiny at the top of the page. What kind of image do you get of the place described in the poem?

....
....
....
....
....

EXAM-STYLE QUESTION **Q3** Compare 'Nothing's Changed' with one other poem in which the poet describes a place that is important to them.

Compare:
- why these places are important to the poets
- what impression the poets give of these places
- how they use poetic devices to create this impression.

EXAM-STYLE QUESTION **Q4** Compare how particular places are shown to be important in 'Hurricane Hits England' and one other poem.

Compare:
- how the poets describe the places
- the ideas and attitudes expressed in the poems
- how the poems make you feel about the places they describe.

Section Two — The Themes

Two Cultures

These Poems are about Two Cultures:

Island Man (pages 6-7)
Search For My Tongue (pages 18-19)
Unrelated Incidents (pages 20-21)
Half-Caste (pages 22-23)
Presents from my Aunts in Pakistan (pages 28-29)
Hurricane Hits England (pages 32-33)

Q1   Do you feel that you belong to just one culture, or to more than one? Explain your answer.

....
....
....
....

Q2   Like you've done on every single page of this section, pick a poem that you've studied from the list above. Does the poet think that the two cultures can mix well or not? Explain your answer.

....
....
....
....
....

EXAM-STYLE QUESTION

Q3   Compare the effect of contrasting cultures in 'Island Man' and one other poem.

Compare:
- whether the different cultures clash or mix together
- the poetic devices used to show the contrast
- the feelings and attitudes shown by the contrast.

EXAM-STYLE QUESTION

Q4   Compare 'Presents from my Aunts in Pakistan' to another poem that involves a conflict of two cultures.

Compare:
- the ways the different cultures are described
- how the poets present the conflict between cultures
- the poets' feelings about belonging to two cultures.

Section Two — The Themes

Universal Ideas

These Poems are about Universal Ideas:

Nothing's Changed (pages 4-5)
Two Scavengers in a Truck... (pages 10-11)
Vultures (pages 14-15)
Half-Caste (pages 22-23)
Love After Love (pages 24-25)
This Room (pages 26-27)
Hurricane Hits England (pages 32-33)

Q1 Describe a film, TV programme, play or book that you have seen or read that made you think about a particular issue.

....
....
....
....

Q2 Pick a number from 1 to 7. Congratulations, you've just chosen a poem from the box at the top. What is the universal idea in this poem? How does the poet present this idea?

....
....
....
....
....

EXAM-STYLE QUESTION

Q3 'Vultures' deals with the theme of good and evil in humans.
Compare 'Vultures' to one other poem that deals with a universal idea.

Compare:
- the introduction and presentation of ideas
- the attitudes expressed by the poets
- the poets' conclusions.

EXAM-STYLE QUESTION

Q4 Compare the universal ideas in 'Hurricane Hits England' and one other poem.

Compare:
- the ways the poets discuss these ideas in their poems
- the opinions the poets present about these ideas
- how the poets relate these ideas to more specific themes in the poem.

Section Two — The Themes

Traditions

These Poems are about Traditions:

Limbo (pages 2-3)
Night of the Scorpion (pages 12-13)
What Were They Like? (pages 16-17)
Presents from my Aunts in Pakistan (pages 28-29)
Hurricane Hits England (pages 32-33)

Q1 Describe a tradition that you take part in.

....
....
....
....

Q2 OK, I promise this is the last time. Pick a poem from the box and explain what impression the poet gives of the traditions it describes.

....
....
....
....
....

EXAM-STYLE QUESTION **Q3** Compare 'Presents from my Aunts in Pakistan' with one other poem that describes cultural traditions.

Compare:
- the different traditions described
- the poetic devices used to describe the traditions
- whether the poets present these traditions as a good thing or a bad thing.

EXAM-STYLE QUESTION **Q4** Compare the ways traditions are presented in 'Night of the Scorpion' and one other poem.

Compare:
- the language used to describe the traditions
- whether the poet feels a part of these traditions or an outsider to them
- your responses to the traditions described.

Section Two — The Themes

Acknowledgements

The Publisher would like to thank:

Chinua Achebe 'Vultures' from Beware Soul Brother (African Writers, Heinemann Educational, 1972)

Tatamkhulu Afrika 'Nothing's Changed' © Tatamkhulu Afrika

John Agard 'Half Caste' reproduced by kind permission of John Agard c/o Caroline Sheldon Literary Agency from Get Back Pimple (Penguin, 1996).

Moniza Alvi Carrying My Wife, Bloodaxe Books, 2000

Sujata Bhatt 'Search For My Tongue' from Brunizem (1998), reprinted by permission of the publishers, Carcanet Press Ltd.

Edward Kamau Brathwaite 'Limbo' from The Arrivants: A New World Trilogy (OUP, 1973), reprinted by permission of Oxford University Press.

Imtiaz Dharker Postcards from god, Bloodaxe Books, 1997;
I Speak for the Devil, Bloodaxe Books 2001

Nissim Ezekiel 'Night of the Scorpion' from Poverty Poems, reproduced by permission of Oxford University Press India, New Delhi

Lawrence Ferlinghetti 'Two Scavengers in A Truck, Two Beautiful People In A Mercedes' from These Are My Rivers, copyright © 1979 by Lawrence Ferlinghetti. Reprinted by permission of New Directions Publishing Corp.

Tom Leonard 'Unrelated Incidents' © Tom Leonard, from Intimate Voices Etruscan Books, Devon

Denise Levertov 'What Were They Like?' from Selected Poems (Bloodaxe Books, 1986). Reproduced by permission of Pollinger Limited and the proprietor.

Grace Nichols 'Island Man' from The Fat Black Woman's Poems (Virago, 1984), copyright © Grace Nichols 1984, and 'Hurricane Hits England' from Sunrise (Virago, 1996), copyright © Grace Nichols 1996

Niyi Osundare 'Not My Business' from Songs of the Seasons (Heinemann Educational Books, Nigeria, 1990)

Derek Walcott 'Love After Love' from Collected Poems 1948-1984 (1986), Faber and Faber

Photographs:

'Children' With thanks to the District 6 Museum
'Traffic' With thanks to Ian Britton of Freefoto.com

Every effort has been made to locate copyright holders and obtain permission to reproduce poems and photographs. For those poems and photographs where it has been difficult to trace the copyright holder of the work, we would be grateful for information. If any copyright holder would like us to make an amendment to the acknowledgements, please notify us and we will gladly update the book at the next reprint. Thank you.